Dedication

To Kayla, my soul partner,
whose love and unwavering support have guided me on this incredible journey.
Thank you for being my rock, my inspiration, and my confidant. Together, we
illuminate the path of infinite possibilities.

To my children, Naomi, Keegan, Kira Raye, and Donnie III,
you are my greatest joys and the source of boundless love. May you always follow
your hearts, chase your dreams, and embrace the power within you to manifest a
world of wonder.

To my Tio Renaldo and Jeff, and my Aunt Yvonne,
your wisdom, guidance, and endless encouragement have shaped me into the
person I am today. Thank you for being my mentors and for sharing your profound
knowledge.

To Athena, and Vinnie,
your unwavering belief in my potential has fueled my journey. Your love and
presence have given me the strength to embrace my inner divinity and unleash my
creative power.

To my parents, Rest in peace Donald Sr. and Lisa, and Grandma Gloria
you are forever in my heart. Your love and teachings continue to guide me on this
earthly plane. I am eternally grateful for the foundation you provided and the
values you instilled within me.

To my Cousin Jacob,
thank you for your friendship, laughter, and shared adventures. Your unwavering
support has been a constant source of inspiration.

This book is dedicated to all of you, my beloved family and friends. Your love,
presence, and belief in me have been a catalyst for my growth and transformation.
I carry your love within my heart as I embark on this journey to empower others
and unlock the extraordinary power within them.

With heartfelt gratitude and boundless love,
Prime Sanchez
This I know to be true!

ISBN: 9798397549837

Cover design by Canva Creative Studio

Interior design by Apple Pages

Edited by Donald Sanchez

Published by KPD

www.SickDaysVisuals.com

Printed in United States

First Edition: 2023

This book is intended to provide general guidance and information. The author and publisher assume no responsibility for any errors or omissions, or for any outcomes resulting from the use of the information provided in this book. The information contained in this book is not intended to serve as legal, financial, or professional advice. Readers are encouraged to seek the advice of professionals regarding their specific situations.

While every effort has been made to ensure the accuracy and completeness of the information presented in this book, the author and publisher cannot be held liable for any damages or losses arising from the use of this book.

Any resemblance to actual persons, living or dead, or actual events is purely coincidental.

Cover image: Canva Creative Studio

"Within you lies the power to create galaxies, to shape your reality, and to manifest your deepest desires. Embrace the truth that you are the master of your own universe, and watch as the stars align in your favor."

-Prime Sanchez

Prologue

Unlocking Your Inner Universe

This I know to be true! Dear reader, welcome to a journey of self-discovery and empowerment, where you will unlock the secrets of your inner universe and harness the extraordinary power within you. In this introductory chapter, we embark on a quest to explore the depths of your consciousness, understanding that you hold the key to manifesting your dreams and shaping your reality.

Imagine, if you will, a vast cosmos stretching infinitely in every direction. This cosmic canvas represents the boundless potential and possibilities that exist within you. You are the master of your own universe, the creator of your reality, and every thought, belief, and intention serves as the brushstrokes upon this cosmic canvas.

The knowledge that you are about to uncover has been passed down through ancient wisdom, teachings, and the universal principles that govern the very fabric of existence. It is a culmination of insights from spiritual sages, philosophers, and mystics who have delved into the depths of consciousness and uncovered the profound truth that we are all interconnected with the universe.

Throughout this journey, we will transcend the limitations of organized religion and embrace a broader perspective that encompasses the universal truths shared by various spiritual traditions. We will explore the wisdom of Thoth, Hermes Trismegistus, the Kybalion, and the Hermetica, among others, delving into the universal principles that underpin our existence.

At the heart of our exploration lies the understanding that everything in the universe is intricately connected, and that the power to manifest lies within our thoughts and consciousness. By becoming aware of our conscious and unconscious thoughts, we unlock the key to shaping our reality and manifesting our desires.

Through the pages of this book, we will delve into the principles of manifestation, vibrational alignment, and the interplay between the individual and the universe. We will discover how the power of intention and the art of surrendering to the flow of the universe can pave the way for a life of fulfillment, abundance, and purpose.

Dear reader, I invite you to embark on this transformative journey with an open mind and a willingness to explore the depths of your inner universe. Embrace the truth that you hold the power to shape your reality, and that the universe eagerly awaits your command. As we delve into the subsequent chapters, remember that you are not alone on this journey. The universal forces are conspiring in your favor, supporting and guiding you every step of the way.

Are you ready, dear reader, to unlock your inner universe and unleash the extraordinary power that lies within you? Let us embark on this transformative quest together.

This I know to be true!

1

The Universal Mind - Harnessing the Power Within

This I know to be true! In the vast tapestry of existence, the Universal Mind is the cosmic conductor orchestrating the dance of creation. It is the grand symphony of consciousness, the force that breathes life into all that is. Within this infinite sea of energy, your thoughts and consciousness play a pivotal role in shaping the very fabric of your reality.

Let me share with you an awe-inspiring anecdote that will illuminate the profound impact of your thoughts on the canvas of your life.

Imagine yourself standing before a blank canvas, the brush trembling in your hand, and a palette of vibrant colors laid out before you. This moment is an invitation–an invitation to create, to express the deepest yearnings of your soul. As you dip your brush into the colors, a surge of anticipation and excitement rushes through your veins.

With each stroke, you bring forth a piece of your inner world onto the canvas. The canvas becomes a mirror of your thoughts, emotions, and beliefs, transforming into a portal that connects the ethereal realm with the tangible. As you pour your heart into your creation, the colors dance, meld, and intertwine, manifesting a vibrant landscape that reflects the beauty within.

This moment, dear reader, encapsulates the essence of your power–the power to shape your reality through the creative force of your thoughts. Your mind is the brush, and your consciousness the guiding hand that breathes life into the canvas of your life.

But remember, just as an artist must choose their colors with intention, you too must be mindful of the thoughts you entertain. Imagine if doubts, fears, and self-limiting beliefs clouded your vision, staining the canvas with dark hues. The once vibrant landscape would lose its brilliance, and your creation would be marred by shadows.

However, fear not, for within the depths of your being lies an infinite wellspring of potential–a wellspring that can infuse your thoughts with vibrant hues of positivity, gratitude, and limitless possibility. When you consciously choose to embrace empowering thoughts, aligning with the frequency of joy and abundance, the universe responds in kind.

Let me share another powerful anecdote to illustrate the profound influence of consciousness on the physical world.

In the realm of quantum physics, a groundbreaking experiment known as the double-slit experiment unveiled a mind-boggling truth. Scientists discovered that the behavior of particles changed when observed. They found that the mere act of observation collapsed the infinite possibilities into a single outcome. This remarkable revelation demonstrated the profound connection between consciousness and physical reality.

Consider the implications, dear reader. Your consciousness, your very presence as an observer, has the power to shape the behavior of particles. If such a seemingly insignificant act can influence the microscopic realm, imagine the magnitude of your influence on the macrocosmic world–the world that surrounds you.

This anecdote invites you to recognize the immense power within your thoughts and consciousness. As you become aware of this power, you can deliberately direct your thoughts towards the reality you desire. Every thought you think, every word you speak, and every intention you set creates a ripple in the cosmic ocean, influencing the currents of creation.

Now, let me return to the story of Maria, a young woman who dared to awaken to the power of her thoughts and consciousness.

Maria had always dreamed of pursuing a career in music, but the weight of self-doubt and fear held her back for years. She convinced herself that her dream was beyond reach, that she lacked the talent and the opportunities necessary to succeed. Maria's canvas remained blank, devoid of the vibrant hues that could have painted her dreams into existence.

One fateful day, a shift occurred within Maria. She stumbled upon the profound knowledge that her thoughts and beliefs shaped her reality. Inspired by this revelation, she mustered the courage to affirm her belief in her musical talent, to visualize herself performing on grand stages, and to unleash her creativity without restraint.

As Maria changed her inner dialogue, a transformation began to unfold. Miraculous synchronicities emerged–

chance encounters with influential mentors who recognized her potential, invitations to perform at local events that showcased her talent, and serendipitous connections with fellow musicians who became her lifelong collaborators. These were not mere coincidences; they were the direct result of Maria's newfound alignment with her true desires.

Dear reader, Maria's story serves as a powerful reminder that your thoughts possess transformative potential. By harnessing the power of your consciousness, you can shape your reality in awe-inspiring ways. It is through aligning your thoughts, emotions, and intentions with the frequency of your desires that the universe conspires to manifest your dreams.

This I know to be true!

Now that you understand the profound impact of your thoughts and consciousness, it is time to embark on a journey of self-mastery. In the chapters that follow, we will delve deeper into the principles and practices that will empower you to manifest your desires and embrace the life you truly deserve.

Prepare yourself, dear reader, for a transformative exploration of your inner universe. Together, we will unravel the mysteries of conscious creation, tap into the immense power of the Universal Mind, and awaken the dormant potential within you. Brace yourself for a paradigm shift, as you embrace the truth that you are the master of your own universe.

Are you ready to step into your power, dear reader? Let us embark on this remarkable adventure together, for the universe eagerly awaits your command.

This I know to be true!

2

The Interconnected Web of Creation - Unity in Diversity

This I know to be true!

In the intricate tapestry of existence, we are not isolated beings but interconnected threads woven together by the Universal Mind. The diversity of life, with its myriad forms and expressions, is a testament to the limitless creativity of the cosmos. Within this vast interplay of energies, we find the seeds of unity and the power to co-create a harmonious reality.

Let me share with you an inspiring anecdote that will illuminate the profound interconnectedness of all beings.

Picture a majestic forest, a sanctuary of life teeming with trees, plants, and creatures of all kinds. Amidst the vibrant foliage, there stands a towering oak–a symbol of strength, wisdom, and resilience. Beneath its protective branches, a community of organisms thrives in perfect symbiosis.

In this enchanting forest, everything is interconnected. The oak tree, with its sturdy trunk and sprawling branches, provides shelter for birds, squirrels, and countless insects.

Its leaves, kissed by sunlight, absorb carbon dioxide and exhale life-giving oxygen. The roots of the oak extend deep into the earth, intertwining with the intricate network of mycelium, forming a bond that allows the exchange of nutrients and information among plants in the ecosystem.

The forest exemplifies the profound truth that we, too, are interconnected with the world around us. Just as the oak tree and its inhabitants rely on each other for sustenance and support, so too do we rely on the web of relationships that permeates our lives. Each interaction, each moment of connection, is a thread that weaves us into the grand tapestry of existence.

Consider the human body–an awe-inspiring example of interconnectedness. It is a marvel of biological systems working in unison to sustain life. The heart pumps blood, delivering nourishment to every cell. The lungs exchange oxygen and carbon dioxide, enabling the breath of life. The nervous system relays messages, allowing us to move, think, and feel. Each organ, each cell, has its unique function, yet they harmonize, collaborating to create the symphony of the human experience.

In a similar vein, dear reader, the diverse individuals, cultures, and belief systems that populate our world are integral parts of the grand design. Each person carries a unique spark of consciousness, a distinct note in the cosmic orchestra. When we recognize and honor the inherent value of every being, we embrace the interconnectedness that binds us all.

Let me share another poignant anecdote that will illustrate the power of unity in diversity.

Imagine a gathering of individuals from different walks of life–people of varying backgrounds, experiences, and perspectives. At first glance, they may seem disconnected, each pursuing their own paths. But as they come together, something magical happens. They begin to share their stories, their dreams, and their aspirations. In this exchange, barriers crumble, and a tapestry of shared humanity emerges.

As they listen to one another with open hearts, the seeds of understanding take root, and empathy blossoms. Differences are celebrated, for they offer opportunities to learn and grow. From this unity in diversity springs a collective power—a power that can catalyze positive change, foster innovation, and ignite the flame of collective awakening.

Dear reader, within the tapestry of interconnectedness, your thoughts, words, and actions reverberate through the cosmic web. The energy you emit, whether positive or negative, ripples through the collective consciousness, shaping the reality we collectively experience. When you embrace the interconnected nature of existence, you become a conscious participant in the co-creation of a harmonious and thriving world.

This I know to be true!

As you awaken to the truth of our interconnectedness, a profound responsibility arises—a responsibility to honor and uplift one another, to recognize the divine essence that resides within each being. When you choose love over fear, compassion over judgment, and unity over division, you contribute to the symphony of harmony that resounds throughout the cosmos.

Now, let us reflect on the interconnectedness in our own lives. Consider the relationships you have—family, friends, colleagues, and even chance encounters. How can you nurture these connections? How can you contribute to the well-being and growth of others? Remember, dear reader, that even the smallest act of kindness, a single thread of compassion, can have a ripple effect that reverberates far beyond your immediate sphere.

In the chapters that follow, we will explore practices and principles that will empower you to cultivate profound connections, embrace diversity, and harness the power of unity. Together, we will unveil the infinite possibilities that arise when we come together as conscious co-creators in the magnificent tapestry of existence.

Prepare yourself, dear reader, for a transformative exploration of our interconnected web of creation. Let us celebrate our diversity, honor our shared humanity, and embark on a journey that will awaken within us the understanding that we are not separate, but beautifully intertwined.

Are you ready to embrace the power of unity in diversity, dear reader? Let us continue this remarkable journey together, for the interconnected universe eagerly awaits our collective evolution.

This I know to be true!

3

Conscious Co-Creation - Unleashing the Power of Intention

This I know to be true!

Dear reader, within the depths of your being resides a powerful creative force—a force that has the ability to shape your reality and manifest your deepest desires. It is through the art of conscious co-creation that we tap into this innate power and align our thoughts, beliefs, and actions with the limitless possibilities of the universe. In this expanded chapter, we will delve even deeper into the extraordinary power of intention, exploring its essence, practical applications, and the profound impact it can have on every aspect of our lives.

Imagine, if you will, a painter standing before a blank canvas. With a clear vision in mind, the artist sets an intention to create a masterpiece. Each brushstroke becomes a deliberate act of creation, bringing the image to life in vivid detail. This, dear reader, is the essence of conscious co-creation–harnessing the power of intention to shape the world around us.

Intentions are the seeds of manifestation, the starting point of every creative endeavor. When we set a clear and focused intention, we establish a guiding compass that aligns our thoughts, beliefs, and actions with our desired outcome. It is through this alignment that we unlock the immense power within us to shape our reality.

Let me share with you an inspiring anecdote that illustrates the transformative power of conscious co-creation.

Meet Sarah, a woman who had always dreamed of starting her own business but felt trapped by self-doubt and limiting beliefs. One day, Sarah made a conscious decision to harness the power of intention and consciously co-create the reality she desired. She began by clarifying her vision, setting clear and specific goals for her business, and aligning her thoughts and actions with her desired outcome.

As Sarah committed to her vision, she noticed a remarkable shift within herself and in the circumstances that unfolded. She attracted the right opportunities, connected with like-minded individuals who supported her journey, and experienced synchronicities that seemed to guide her every step. Through her focused intention and aligned actions, Sarah's dream business became a tangible reality, exceeding even her own expectations.

Dear reader, conscious co-creation is not a passive endeavor. It is a dynamic and participatory process that requires an unwavering belief in your own creative power and an active engagement in shaping your reality. Let us now explore the transformative power of conscious co-creation in greater depth:

1.   Clarifying Intentions: The journey of conscious co-creation begins with clarity of intention. Take a moment to reflect on what you truly desire in life. What is your vision? What are your goals? Write them down with as much detail as possible. By defining what you want to manifest, you create a clear pathway for the universe to align with your intentions.

2.   Aligning Thoughts and Beliefs: Thoughts and beliefs shape our reality. To harness the power of conscious co-creation, it is essential to examine and transform any limiting beliefs that may hinder our creative potential. Become aware of any negative self-talk or doubts that arise. Replace them with positive affirmations and empowering beliefs that support your intentions. Affirm to yourself daily that you are deserving and capable of manifesting your desires.

3.   Inspired Action: Intentions without action remain mere dreams. Conscious co-creation involves taking inspired action towards your intentions. This means actively seeking opportunities, following your intuition, and stepping out of your comfort zone. Stay open and receptive to the signs and synchronicities that guide you along your path. Trust your inner guidance and act upon it, for it is through inspired action that you align yourself with the flow of creation.

4.   Trusting the Process: Trust is an essential element of conscious co-creation. It is the unwavering faith that the universe is conspiring in your favor and working tirelessly to bring your intentions to fruition. Trust that the timing is always perfect, even if things don't unfold

exactly as you imagined. Release the need for control and surrender to the wisdom of the universe. Have faith that everything is happening for your highest good, and allow the magic of co-creation to unfold in its own beautiful way.

As you embark on your journey of conscious co-creation, dear reader, remember that intention is not just a one-time declaration. It is a continuous and evolving process. Regularly review and reaffirm your intentions, staying true to your vision even in the face of challenges. Be patient, persistent, and unwavering in your belief in the power of your intentions.

Embrace the truth that you are a co-creator of your reality, dear reader, and that the universe eagerly awaits your intentions. When you align your thoughts, beliefs, and actions with your desires, you tap into the limitless creative potential that resides within you.

Unleash the power of intention, dear reader, and witness the miraculous transformation that unfolds as you consciously co-create your reality.

This I know to be true!

4

The Dance of Surrender - Trusting the Flow of the Universe

This I know to be true!

Within the intricate tapestry of the universe, there is a subtle dance—a dance of surrender. It is the dance of letting go and trusting in the flow of life. In this chapter, we will delve deeper into the profound concept of surrender and explore how it allows us to harmonize with the rhythm of the universe, bringing us greater peace, serenity, and fulfillment.

Imagine, dear reader, standing at the edge of a majestic waterfall. As you gaze at the cascading water, you witness its effortless descent, surrendering to gravity's pull. The water does not resist or try to control its path; it simply flows with grace and ease. In this surrender, it finds its true power.

In much the same way, surrender is not a sign of weakness or passivity, but rather an act of profound strength and wisdom. It is the recognition that there are forces greater than us, and by aligning ourselves with these forces, we unlock a reservoir of guidance, support, and infinite possibilities.

Let me share with you an inspiring anecdote that exemplifies the transformative power of surrender.

Meet Sarah, a determined and ambitious individual who had always believed that success was solely the result of hard work and relentless effort. Sarah would meticulously plan and control every aspect of her life, convinced that this was the path to achievement.

However, despite her tireless efforts, Sarah found herself feeling drained, overwhelmed, and disconnected from the joy of living. It was in this state of exhaustion that she stumbled upon the concept of surrender.

Reluctantly, Sarah decided to experiment with surrendering control and trusting in the flow of the universe. She started by relinquishing her attachment to outcomes and instead focused on aligning her intentions and taking inspired action. She learned to release the need to micromanage every detail and allowed herself to be guided by a greater intelligence.

To her surprise, Sarah discovered a newfound sense of freedom, serenity, and synchronicity in her life. Doors began to open effortlessly, and she encountered unexpected opportunities and connections. Sarah realized that by surrendering the need for control and trusting in the wisdom of the universe, she had tapped into a limitless source of support and guidance.

Dear reader, surrender is not about resigning ourselves to fate or relinquishing our dreams; it is about finding the delicate balance between intention and detachment. It is about aligning ourselves with the flow of the universe, trusting that there is a divine order at work, and having faith that everything is unfolding as it should.

Now, let us explore the transformative power of surrender in greater depth:

1. Letting Go of Resistance: Surrender begins by releasing resistance and accepting the present moment as it is. It is an invitation to embrace what is, rather than constantly striving for what could be. By surrendering resistance, we open ourselves to new possibilities and a deeper sense of peace.

2. Trusting Divine Timing: Surrender involves trusting in divine timing and allowing life to unfold at its own pace. It requires us to relinquish our need for control and have faith that everything is happening in perfect alignment with our highest good. Trusting the process allows us to let go of anxiety and embrace a state of flow and ease.

3. Cultivating Detachment: Surrender asks us to cultivate detachment from outcomes and detach our sense of self-worth from external achievements. It is the understanding that our true value lies in our essence, not in external validation. By releasing attachment, we free ourselves from the limitations of ego and open ourselves to greater joy and fulfillment.

4. Embracing Faith and Intuition: Surrender is an invitation to listen to our inner guidance and trust our intuition. It requires us to let go of the need for logic and control and instead surrender to the wisdom of our hearts. By embracing faith and intuition, we tap into a wellspring of inner knowing and align ourselves

with the cosmic dance of the universe.

Dear reader, as you embark on the path of surrender, remember that it is a continuous practice–an ever-evolving dance. It is not a one-time event but a way of being–a way of aligning ourselves with the vast intelligence of the universe. Surrender allows us to release the burden of control and step into a state of harmony and co-creation.

As we conclude this chapter, I invite you to reflect upon the concept of surrender in your own life. Are there areas where you can release resistance and trust in the greater flow of the universe? How can you cultivate a deeper sense of surrender and embrace the wisdom that comes with letting go?

Embrace the dance of surrender, dear reader, and witness the miracles that unfold when you surrender to the benevolent rhythm of the universe.

This I know to be true!

5

Embracing the Power of Gratitude - Cultivating Abundance and Joy

This I know to be true!

Gratitude, dear reader, is a transformative force that has the power to illuminate our lives and invite boundless abundance and joy. In this chapter, we will delve into the profound practice of gratitude and explore how it opens the floodgates of blessings, shifts our perspective, and allows us to experience the fullness of life.

Imagine, if you will, a radiant sunrise painting the sky with hues of gold and pink. As you witness this breathtaking spectacle, a deep sense of gratitude washes over you. In that moment, you are fully present, appreciating the beauty and wonder that surrounds you. This, dear reader, is the power of gratitude– the ability to infuse our lives with awe and appreciation for the blessings, both big and small.

Let me share with you an inspiring anecdote that illustrates the transformative power of gratitude.

Meet Michael, a man who had spent most of his life chasing external success and accumulating material possessions. Despite his achievements, he felt a persistent emptiness within, as if something vital was missing from his life. It was during a moment of introspection that Michael stumbled upon the practice of gratitude.

With a sense of curiosity, Michael decided to embark on a gratitude journey. Each day, he committed to reflecting on the blessings in his life and expressing heartfelt gratitude for them. From the simple joys of a warm cup of coffee in the morning to the love and support of his family and friends, Michael recognized the abundance that surrounded him.

As he deepened his practice, Michael noticed a profound shift within himself. The more he cultivated gratitude, the more blessings seemed to flow into his life. He experienced a newfound sense of contentment, joy, and connection with others. It was as if gratitude had unlocked a hidden reservoir of abundance that had always been present but had gone unnoticed.

Dear reader, the power of gratitude lies not in denying life's challenges but in shifting our perspective and focusing on the blessings that exist amidst adversity. Let us explore the transformative power of gratitude in greater depth:

1. Shifting Perspective: Gratitude invites us to shift our perspective from lack to abundance, from despair to hope. It is a gentle reminder that even in the face of challenges, there is always something to be grateful for. By redirecting our attention to the blessings in our lives, we elevate our vibration and invite more positivity and abundance.

2. Cultivating Appreciation: Gratitude is the practice of intentionally appreciating the present moment and acknowledging the gifts that life bestows upon us. It is about savoring the simple pleasures, expressing appreciation for others, and recognizing the interconnectedness of all beings. Through appreciation, we deepen our connection to the web of life and open ourselves to infinite possibilities.

3. Magnetizing Abundance: Gratitude acts as a powerful magnet, drawing in more of what we appreciate into our lives. As we focus our attention on the blessings we have, we signal to the universe that we are open to receiving more abundance. It is a beautiful cycle of gratitude and manifestation, where the more we express gratitude, the more abundance we attract.

4. Cultivating Joy and Well-Being: Gratitude is a gateway to joy and well-being. When we cultivate an attitude of gratitude, we shift our energy to a positive state, uplifting our emotions and overall well-being. It allows us to cultivate resilience in the face of adversity and embrace a more fulfilling and joyous life.

Dear reader, as you reflect upon the power of gratitude, I encourage you to embark on your own gratitude journey. Take a moment each day to pause and appreciate the blessings that grace your life. Whether it's the laughter of loved ones, the beauty of nature, or the simple pleasures that bring you joy, let gratitude be your guiding light.

Embrace the transformative power of gratitude, and watch as it cultivates abundance, joy, and a profound sense of interconnectedness in your life.

This I know to be true!

6

The Power of Self-Love - Embracing Your Inner Divinity

This I know to be true!

Within the depths of your being, dear reader, lies a wellspring of love and divinity waiting to be embraced. In this chapter, we will explore the profound power of self-love and how it enables us to recognize and honor our inherent worthiness. By cultivating a deep and unconditional love for ourselves, we awaken our inner divinity and radiate that love outward, transforming our lives and the world around us. Imagine, if you will, a garden blooming with vibrant flowers of every color. As you walk through this enchanting sanctuary, you notice a single flower standing tall amidst the rest—the flower of self-love. It emanates a radiant glow, captivating your heart and soul. This, dear reader, is the essence of self-love—the ability to embrace and nurture the divinity that resides within us.

Let me share with you an inspiring anecdote that illustrates the transformative power of self-love.

Meet Maya, a woman who had spent much of her life seeking validation and acceptance from others. She had believed that her worth was dependent on external factors—her appearance, achievements, and the opinions of others. However, Maya reached a turning point when she realized that true happiness and fulfillment could only be found within.

With a newfound determination, Maya embarked on a journey of self-love. She began to treat herself with compassion, kindness, and acceptance. Maya recognized her strengths, celebrated her accomplishments, and embraced her flaws as part of her unique journey. She learned to set boundaries, honor her needs, and prioritize her well-being. In doing so, Maya unleashed a wellspring of love that transformed her life.

As Maya's love for herself grew, she noticed profound shifts in her relationships, career, and overall sense of fulfillment. She attracted healthier connections that reflected her newfound self-worth. Maya pursued her passions with unwavering confidence, leading her to new opportunities and achievements. The world around her responded to her inner radiance, mirroring the love she had cultivated within herself.

Dear reader, self-love is not a selfish act, but a sacred responsibility—a commitment to honor and cherish the divine essence that resides within each of us. Let us explore the transformative power of self-love in greater depth:

1. Acceptance and Compassion: Self-love begins with radical acceptance and compassion for ourselves. It is the willingness to embrace our strengths and weaknesses, to forgive ourselves for past mistakes, and to treat ourselves with gentleness and understanding. Through acceptance, we create space for growth and transformation.

2. Nurturing Well-Being: Self-love invites us to prioritize our well-being on all levels—physical,

emotional, and spiritual. It is the recognition that we are deserving of love, care, and nourishment. By prioritizing self-care rituals, healthy boundaries, and practices that nurture our soul, we honor our divinity and create a foundation of resilience and vitality.

3. Unleashing Authenticity: Self-love encourages us to embrace our authenticity and honor our true desires and passions. It is the permission to live life on our own terms, free from the expectations and judgments of others. By unleashing our authentic selves, we create a life that is aligned with our soul's purpose and experience true fulfillment.

4. Radiating Love: Self-love is a powerful force that radiates outward, transforming not only our own lives but also the lives of those around us. As we cultivate love within ourselves, we become beacons of light, inspiring others to embrace their own divinity. By loving ourselves, we contribute to the collective awakening and create a ripple effect of love and compassion.

Dear reader, as you reflect upon the power of self-love, I invite you to embark on a sacred journey of embracing your inner divinity. Shower yourself with love, kindness, and acceptance. Celebrate your unique beauty and worthiness. Honor your dreams, passions, and desires. Embrace the truth that you are deserving of love, joy, and abundance.
Embrace the transformative power of self-love and witness how it unfolds as a sacred gift in your life.
This I know to be true!

7

The Power of Intention - Manifesting Your Desires with Clarity and Purpose

This I know to be true!

Dear reader, within the depths of your being lies a wellspring of creative power–an extraordinary force that can bring your deepest desires into physical manifestation. It is through the power of intention that we unlock this creative potential and set in motion the process of manifesting our dreams with clarity and purpose. In this expanded chapter, we will delve even deeper into the profound power of intention, exploring its essence, practical applications, and the transformative impact it can have on every aspect of your life.

Imagine, if you will, standing at the edge of a vast ocean. With a heart full of clarity and purpose, you set an intention to sail towards your dreams. Each choice you make, each action you take, becomes a deliberate step towards manifesting your desires. This, dear reader, is the essence of the power of intention–harnessing your inner compass to guide you towards the life you envision.

Intentions are the energetic blueprints that shape our reality. When we set a clear and focused intention, we activate a powerful force within us, aligning our thoughts, beliefs, and actions with the desired outcome. It is through this alignment that we ignite the creative forces of the universe and invite synchronicities and opportunities to support our journey.

Let me share with you an inspiring anecdote that illustrates the transformative power of intention.

Meet Michael, a man who had always dreamed of traveling the world and immersing himself in different cultures. However, his dream seemed distant and unattainable. One day, Michael made a profound shift in his mindset and decided to harness the power of intention to manifest his desires. He created a detailed vision board, filled with images of the places he wished to visit, and infused it with the energy of excitement and gratitude.

As Michael focused on his intentions and took inspired action, remarkable synchronicities began to unfold. He met a travel enthusiast who became his mentor and shared valuable tips and resources. Unexpected opportunities for work and volunteer experiences in foreign countries presented themselves. With each step, Michael's dream became more tangible, and he eventually embarked on a transformative journey that exceeded his wildest expectations.

Dear reader, the power of intention is not just a whimsical notion or a fleeting thought. It is a deliberate and conscious choice to align your entire being with the manifestation of your desires. Let us now explore the transformative power of intention in greater depth:

1. Clarity of Desires: Begin by gaining clarity on what you truly desire to manifest in your life. Take the time

to reflect on your passions, dreams, and aspirations. Write them down in vivid detail, allowing yourself to fully immerse in the emotions and sensations that accompany the realization of your desires. The more precise and specific your intentions, the clearer the signal you send to the universe.

2. Amplifying Beliefs: Your beliefs shape your reality and influence your ability to manifest your desires. Examine any limiting beliefs that may be holding you back and replace them with empowering ones. Affirmations, visualizations, and positive self-talk can help you shift your beliefs and align them with your intentions. Embrace the belief that you are deserving of all that you desire and that the universe is abundant and supportive.

3. Setting the Stage: Create a sacred space or ritual to set your intentions. This can be as simple as lighting a candle, meditating, or writing in a journal. Engage all your senses in the process and infuse your intentions with positive emotions. Feel the excitement, joy, and gratitude as if your desires have already manifested. This energetic charge strengthens the connection between your intentions and the universal forces.

4. Inspired Action: Intentions alone are not enough; they must be accompanied by inspired action. Take meaningful steps towards your desires, guided by your intuition and the opportunities that present themselves. Trust in the process and be open to the signs and synchronicities that guide you along your path. Embrace the journey with a sense of curiosity

and adventure, knowing that each step brings you closer to your manifestations.

5.   Surrender and Trust: The final step in the dance of intention is surrendering the need for control and trusting in the divine timing of the universe. Detach from the outcome and release any expectations or limitations. Allow the universe to orchestrate the details and bring your intentions to fruition in the most magical and unexpected ways. Trust that the universe is conspiring in your favor and that everything is unfolding as it should.

Dear reader, as you harness the power of intention and align your thoughts, beliefs, and actions with your desires, you activate the inherent creative forces that reside within you. Embrace the clarity and purpose that intention brings, and watch as your dreams manifest in beautiful and awe-inspiring ways.

This I know to be true!

8

Embracing the Flow - Surrendering to the Universe's Guidance

This I know to be true!

Dear reader, within the ebb and flow of life, there is a guiding current—a universal force that is constantly nudging us towards our highest good. It is in surrendering to this divine flow that we open ourselves to the infinite wisdom and guidance of the universe. In this expanded chapter, we will delve even deeper into the profound practice of surrender, exploring its essence, practical applications, and the transformative impact it can have on our lives.

Imagine, if you will, a river meandering through a lush landscape. The river follows the path of least resistance, effortlessly carving its way through obstacles, always moving towards its destination. This, dear reader, is the essence of surrender—trusting in the divine current and allowing it to carry us towards our desired destination.

Surrender does not imply passivity or giving up control. It is an active and conscious choice to release resistance and align ourselves with the natural flow of the universe. It is an invitation to let go of our need for certainty and control, and instead, trust in the unfolding of divine timing and guidance.

Let me share with you an inspiring anecdote that illustrates the transformative power of surrender.

Meet Emily, a young woman who had meticulously planned every aspect of her life. She was determined to follow a specific career path, marry at a certain age, and achieve a particular level of success. However, despite her best efforts, she encountered numerous obstacles and setbacks that left her feeling frustrated and exhausted.

One day, Emily reached a breaking point and realized that her relentless need for control was hindering her growth and happiness. She made a conscious decision to surrender to the flow of the universe, trusting that there was a greater plan in motion. She released her grip on her predetermined outcomes and instead focused on aligning her thoughts and actions with the present moment.

As Emily surrendered to the guidance of the universe, remarkable synchronicities began to occur. She discovered new opportunities that she had never considered before, met inspiring individuals who became her mentors, and found herself in situations that led to unexpected growth and fulfillment. By surrendering to the flow, Emily's life took on a new sense of ease, joy, and purpose.

Dear reader, surrender is not about relinquishing control or giving up on our desires. It is about relinquishing attachment to the specific outcomes and allowing the universe to guide us towards the highest expression of our intentions. Let us now explore the transformative power of surrender in greater depth:

1. Releasing Resistance: Surrender begins with the recognition of resistance–the inner turmoil that arises

when we try to control every aspect of our lives. Become aware of the areas in which you are resisting, whether it be in relationships, career, or personal growth. Let go of the need to control every outcome and release any attachment to how things should be. Embrace the idea that the universe has a grander plan for you.

2. Trusting Divine Timing: Trust that the universe has perfect timing and that everything unfolds according to a higher plan. Embrace patience and surrender the need for instant gratification. Trust that the universe knows the precise moment to bring your desires into fruition. Surrender to the divine timing and remain open to the possibilities that present themselves along the way.

3. Listening to Intuition: Surrendering to the flow requires attuning to your inner voice, your intuition. Quiet the noise of external influences and connect with the wisdom that resides within you. Practice mindfulness and meditation to cultivate a deeper connection with your intuition. Trust the nudges and guidance that arise from within, for they are the whispers of the universe guiding you towards your highest good.

4. Letting Go of Control: Surrendering to the flow means relinquishing control and embracing the notion that there are forces at play beyond our comprehension. Release the illusion of control and surrender the outcomes to the universe. Allow yourself to be guided by the currents of life, knowing

that every experience holds valuable lessons and growth opportunities.

5.   Embracing Faith: Surrender is an act of faith—a deep knowing that the universe is conspiring in your favor. Embrace faith in the unseen, in the magic that exists beyond the limitations of the rational mind. Trust that the universe has your best interests at heart and is continuously guiding you towards your highest potential. Surrendering to the flow requires a leap of faith, but the rewards are immeasurable.

Dear reader, as you surrender to the guidance of the universe, you open yourself to a world of limitless possibilities and effortless alignment. Embrace the flow, let go of resistance, and allow the current of the universe to carry you towards your dreams.

This I know to be true!

9

The Power of Resilience - Embracing Challenges and Cultivating Inner Strength

This I know to be true!

Dear reader, life is a tapestry woven with both joyous moments and challenging trials. It is in the face of adversity that the power of resilience shines brightest—a deep wellspring of inner strength that allows us to navigate through life's challenges with grace and fortitude. In this expanded chapter, we will dive even deeper into the transformative power of resilience, exploring its essence, practical applications, and the profound impact it can have on our lives.

Imagine, if you will, a majestic oak tree standing tall amidst a fierce storm. Though its branches may sway and its leaves may be stripped away, its roots run deep, anchoring it firmly to the earth. This, dear reader, is the essence of resilience—our ability to remain grounded and steadfast in the face of adversity, to bend without breaking.

Resilience is not about avoiding challenges or denying our emotions. It is about embracing the difficulties of life and using them as stepping stones for growth and transformation. It is the capacity to bounce back, to adapt, and to cultivate inner strength amidst the storms of life.

Let me share with you an inspiring anecdote that illustrates the transformative power of resilience.

Meet Sarah, a woman who faced numerous setbacks and obstacles on her path to achieving her dream of becoming an accomplished musician. She encountered rejection, criticism, and self-doubt at every turn. However, Sarah chose to view these challenges as opportunities for growth rather than reasons to give up. She cultivated resilience by maintaining a positive mindset, seeking support from loved ones, and staying committed to her passion.

Through her journey, Sarah experienced immense personal and artistic growth. She developed a deep sense of self-belief, honed her skills through practice and dedication, and eventually achieved remarkable success in her musical career. Sarah's story serves as a testament to the transformative power of resilience, reminding us that challenges can be catalysts for personal and professional triumph.

Dear reader, resilience is not a trait that is bestowed upon a select few. It is a skill that can be cultivated and strengthened over time. Let us now explore the transformative power of resilience in greater depth:

1.   Embracing Adversity: Resilience begins with a shift in perspective. Embrace challenges as opportunities for growth, knowing that they hold valuable lessons and insights. Recognize that adversity is an inevitable part of life's journey and that it is through facing and overcoming challenges that we build resilience.

2.   Nurturing a Positive Mindset: Cultivate a positive and optimistic mindset, even in the face of adversity.

Practice reframing negative thoughts into empowering ones, focusing on solutions rather than problems. Surround yourself with positive influences, affirmations, and inspirational materials that uplift and motivate you.

3.　Building Supportive Relationships: Seek support from loved ones, mentors, and like-minded individuals who can offer guidance and encouragement during difficult times. Connect with a community or support network that understands and empathizes with your experiences. Lean on these relationships for emotional support and a sense of belonging.

4.　Self-Care and Well-being: Nurture your physical, mental, and emotional well-being. Engage in self-care practices that rejuvenate and replenish your energy. Prioritize activities that bring you joy, relaxation, and peace. Take time for rest, reflection, and self-reflection.

5.　Cultivating Inner Strength: Develop a deep sense of inner strength by tapping into your core values and beliefs. Connect with your inner wisdom and intuition, trusting in your ability to overcome challenges. Practice mindfulness, meditation, and self-reflection to cultivate a strong and resilient inner foundation.

Dear reader, as you cultivate the power of resilience within you, you will discover an unwavering strength that carries you through life's challenges. Embrace adversity as an opportunity for growth, nurture a positive mindset, and surround yourself with supportive relationships. By embracing the power of resilience, you will navigate life's storms with grace, wisdom, and inner strength.

This I know to be true!

10

Embracing Abundance and Well-being: Cultivating a Prosperous Mindset

This I know to be true!

Dear reader, within the vast expanse of the universe, abundance is woven into the very fabric of existence. It is our birthright to experience abundance and well-being in all aspects of our lives. In this expanded chapter, we will explore the transformative power of embracing abundance, delving deeper into the practices and mindset necessary to cultivate a prosperous and fulfilling life.

Imagine, if you will, a garden flourishing with vibrant flowers, lush foliage, and an abundance of fruits and vegetables. The garden receives ample sunlight, nourishing rain, and the care of a devoted gardener. This, dear reader, is a metaphor for the abundance that is available to us all. With the right mindset and nurturing, we too can create a bountiful garden of abundance and well-being in our lives.

Embracing abundance begins with adopting a prosperous mindset—a state of consciousness that recognizes and aligns with the infinite possibilities and resources that surround us. It is a shift in perception, moving from scarcity and lack to a mindset of abundance and prosperity. Let me share with you an inspiring anecdote that illustrates the transformative power of embracing abundance.

Meet Alex, a young entrepreneur who started a small business with a grand vision. In the beginning, Alex struggled with feelings of scarcity and limitation. Fearful of competition and financial insecurity, they operated from a place of lack, constantly worried about not having enough. However, Alex realized that this mindset was holding them back from realizing their true potential.

With a shift in consciousness, Alex began to embrace the abundance mindset. They started seeing opportunities where others saw obstacles, viewing setbacks as lessons in disguise. Alex adopted gratitude as a daily practice, acknowledging and appreciating the abundance already present in their life. They cultivated a sense of worthiness, believing that they deserved success and prosperity.

As Alex aligned their thoughts, beliefs, and actions with abundance, remarkable shifts began to occur. New clients and collaborations emerged, financial abundance flowed effortlessly, and Alex's business expanded beyond their wildest dreams. By embracing abundance, Alex not only transformed their business but also experienced profound personal growth and well-being.

Dear reader, cultivating a prosperous mindset and embracing abundance is within your reach. Let us now explore the transformative power of embracing abundance and well-being in greater depth:

1.   Shifting from Scarcity to Abundance: Release scarcity thinking and shift your focus towards abundance. Recognize that the universe is infinitely abundant and that there is more than enough for everyone. Challenge limiting beliefs and replace them with empowering thoughts that affirm abundance in all areas of your life.

2.   Practicing Gratitude: Cultivate a daily practice of gratitude to amplify the abundance already present in your life. Acknowledge and appreciate the blessings, big and small. By focusing on what you are grateful for, you attract more reasons to be grateful.

3.   Visualization and Affirmations: Use the power of visualization and affirmations to program your mind for abundance. Create vivid mental images of your desired outcomes and affirm them with positive statements in the present tense. Visualize yourself already experiencing the abundance and well-being you desire, and feel the emotions associated with it.

4.   Taking Inspired Action: Embrace the co-creative process by taking inspired action towards your goals and desires. Trust your intuition and follow the guidance that arises from within. Act on opportunities that align with your vision and believe in your ability to manifest abundance.

5.   Cultivating a Generous Spirit: Embrace a spirit of generosity and abundance by giving freely and joyfully. Share your time, resources, and talents with others. As you give, you create a positive energetic flow that

attracts more abundance into your life.

Dear reader, as you embrace abundance and cultivate a prosperous mindset, you will align with the infinite possibilities and resources of the universe. Abundance and well-being are your birthright, and by consciously aligning with this truth, you will create a life that is rich, fulfilling, and overflowing with prosperity.

This I know to be true!

Conclusion

Embracing Your Mastery, Shaping Your Universe

Dear reader,

As we come to the end of this transformative journey, I want to commend you for your unwavering commitment to discovering the power within you. Throughout these chapters, we have explored the profound principles that guide us as conscious co-creators of our reality. We have delved into the depths of intention, consciousness, resilience, surrender, and abundance, unraveling the mysteries that lie at the heart of our existence.

You have been initiated into a new way of perceiving yourself and the world around you. You have embraced the wisdom of ancient teachings and the insights of modern thought leaders. But, most importantly, you have recognized that the true power lies within you–the power to shape your universe.

The journey of becoming the master of your own universe is not without its challenges. It requires courage, self-reflection, and an unwavering belief in your inherent worthiness. It demands that you release the limitations of old conditioning, transcend the boundaries of societal expectations, and tap into the limitless potential that resides within you.

But dear reader, I assure you that the journey is worth it. As you step into your mastery, you will witness the incredible transformation that unfolds in every aspect of your life. You will manifest your desires, co-create synchronicities, and experience a profound sense of purpose and fulfillment.

Remember, dear reader, that you are connected to a universal intelligence that is conspiring in your favor. The universe is always listening, responding to the vibrations of your thoughts, emotions, and intentions. You have the power to shape your reality, to manifest your dreams, and to live a life that aligns with your highest potential.

As you close this book and embark on the next chapter of your journey, I invite you to embrace your mastery fully. Trust in the wisdom that resides within you, for it is the compass that will guide you on your path. Be courageous in your intentions, for they have the power to transform the world around you. And above all, remember that you are the master of your universe, a divine being capable of creating miracles.

Dear reader, I am honored to have been your guide on this extraordinary quest for self-discovery and empowerment. Know that the universe celebrates your choice to embark on this journey of awakening and manifestation.

Now, take a moment to bask in the radiance of your own brilliance. Embrace the truth that you are the master of your own universe. Let the knowledge you have gained permeate every fiber of your being and propel you forward on the path of conscious creation.

With boundless love and infinite possibilities, safe travels on your journey to infinity!

Thank you, Prime.

This I know to be true!

About the Author

Prime is a passionate seeker of universal truths and a dedicated explorer of the human consciousness. With a deep curiosity for the mysteries of the universe, Prime has spent a lifetime delving into ancient wisdom, metaphysics, and the principles that underpin our existence.

Inspired by the works of Thoth, Hermes Trismegistus, the Kybalion, and the Hermetica, among others, Prime has synthesized a profound understanding of the interconnectedness of all things and the power of the human mind to shape reality.

Through personal experiences and a continuous quest for knowledge, Prime has embraced the belief that each individual is the master of their own universe, capable of manifesting their deepest desires and unlocking the extraordinary power within.

As an author, Prime seeks to bridge the gap between spirituality and practicality, providing readers with a roadmap to transcend the limitations of organized religion and tap into the universal principles that govern our existence. By drawing upon insights from various spiritual traditions and weaving them into a cohesive narrative, Prime empowers readers to embark on a transformative journey of self-discovery and conscious co-creation.

Prime's writings are a testament to the belief that the power to manifest lies within each individual. Through the exploration of topics such as intention, surrender, resilience, and abundance, Prime guides readers toward unlocking their inner potential and embracing a life of purpose, fulfillment, and joy.

With a compassionate and empathetic approach, Prime's words resonate deeply with agnostics and atheists seeking answers beyond the confines of traditional religious frameworks. By providing practical tools, profound insights, and inspiring anecdotes, Prime empowers readers to embrace their role as the masters of their own universes.

When Prime is not immersed in writing and contemplation, they enjoy spending time in nature, practicing mindfulness and meditation, and engaging in conversations that explore the depths of human consciousness. With an unwavering commitment to personal growth and the upliftment of humanity, Prime continues to inspire and guide others on their transformative journeys.

Through their work, Prime invites readers to step into their true power, unlock the secrets of the universe within, and embrace a reality filled with abundance, joy, and profound purpose.

This I know to be true!

Made in the USA
Columbia, SC
19 June 2023